Original title:

Bloom in the Dark

Author: Henry Beaumont

ISBN HARDBACK: 978-1-80581-833-5

ISBN PAPERBACK: 978-1-80581-360-6

ISBN EBOOK: 978-1-80581-833-5

Drifting in the Night's Embrace

In shadows deep, the moonlight grins,
A cat on a fence, with plans for sins.
Whispers of night dance in the breeze,
Socks on the line catch cool, frosty tease.

A party of fireflies, buzzing in glee,
They've brought snacks, oh what a spree!
Each little flicker, a giggling sprite,
Under the stars, they dance in the night.

Hues of the Hidden

In the garden, a rogue radish twirls,
Twirling and spinning, fame it unfurls.
With carrots in shades of bright orange and green,
They plan a parade, oh what a scene!

Onions are crying, but they can't be sad,
For in their layers, there's laughter they've had.
A cabbage in costume, dressed up for fun,
Under the moon, their revelry's begun.

Solace in the Shadows

Amidst the dusk, a raccoon appears,
Wearing a mask like he's pulling cheers.
Sipping on soda, a bandit at heart,
Stealing the snacks, he's playing his part.

With owls on the prowl, they huddle in delight,
Trading gossip 'bout the silliest fright.
Who's afraid of ghosts? Not these sharp-witted fools,
Laughter erupts, breaking all of their rules.

Sundown Revelations

As day turns to dusk, the crickets take flight,
With a beat so wild, under soft twilight.
A hedgehog with style, struts down the lane,
Wearing a bowtie, he's ready for fame.

The sun bids farewell with a wink and a grin,
Stars start to twinkle; let the games begin!
Each shadow holds secrets, each laugh a new tale,
In the web of the night, all worries set sail.

The Night's Verdant Embrace

In shadows deep the plants have fun,
They giggle softly, 'Look, we've won!'
Winking at the stars so bright,
They dance beneath the silver light.

With every breeze, a chuckle flows,
The leaves are chatting, who really knows?
In this secret garden's cheer,
They've found a way to persevere!

Growth Against the Grain

A cactus claims the sandy night,
With prickly jokes that poke and bite.
He lifts his arms up to the sky,
'I'm sharp but funny, give it a try!'

The mushrooms giggle, 'Here we grow!'
With tiny hats, they steal the show.
In mismatched socks, they prance about,
Rooted deep but filled with clout!

Hope in the Midnight Haze

A daisy dreams of moonlit cheers,
While whistling tunes in quiet years.
'Who needs the sun to get a tan?'
She chuckles at the garden plan!

With petals dressed in shades of blue,
She sprinkles laughter, just a few.
In twilight's grin, they find their fate,
A party grows — just wait, just wait!

Shrouded in Silhouettes

In silhouettes, the flowers tease,
'Can you see us swaying with ease?'
They sway and laugh in midnight's glee,
Beneath a tree, so wild and free!

The moonbeams wink, 'You're doing great!'
While lilacs plan a dubious date.
Whispers float on evening's breeze,
'Let's wear our quirks like fancy frieze!'

The Enigma of Nighttime Blooms

In shadows where the giggles grow,
Mischief dances, putting on a show.
Flowers with a wink, they start to sway,
Undercover blooms, having their play.

The moon looks down with a cheeky grin,
As petals plot where the fun begins.
They sprout in the dark, oh what a sight,
Sneaky blossoms having a late-night flight.

Laughter spills like confetti bright,
Whispers of petals in the soft moonlight.
Each leaf a joker, each stem a jest,
In the garden's laughter, we all feel blessed.

So if you wander beneath the night,
Look for the blooms in their jolly flight.
For in every shadow, there's a tune,
Where flowers frolic 'neath the laughing moon.

Life's Colors in the Night

Under the starry canvas of fright,
Colors pop out, oh what a delight!
Purple giggles and yellow grins,
Nighttime antics where the fun begins.

A daffodil dons a zany hat,
Twirling round a sleepy cat.
With stardust sprinkled on their cheeks,
They spin and dance, playing hide and seek.

A rose gives a wink, oh so sly,
While daisies chuckle and puff up high.
Life's a carnival in the black,
Where colors collide and laughter won't hack.

So join the fun in the moonlit park,
Chasing the hues that ignite the dark.
In this whimsical night, take your stand,
For life's vibrant colors are all quite grand.

In Darkness, They Rise

In shadowy corners, they stretch and sway,
Finding a way to play hide and seek each day.
With petals like secrets, they whisper and laugh,
Always awake while the world takes a nap.

Chasing the moonlight, they dance and twirl,
Wearing their fragrance like a magical pearl.
With roots in the muck but heads in the stars,
They throw midnight parties – bring your own jars!

The Secret Life of Night Flowers

At dusk they convene, a curious crew,
Plotting their mischief and what they will do.
They giggle and sway, with no one to see,
Kicking off shoes, feeling utterly free.

Their colors are bold - a vibrant display,
Confetti of petals that fade into gray.
As crickets provide the DJ's sweet tune,
They jig like there's sugar hidden in the moon.

Surviving the Umbra

When sunlight is snoozing, they take the stage,
Writing their stories, unwritten on page.
In between shadows, they find their delight,
Joking with fireflies, why not? It feels right.

They drink up the stars like a fizzy soft drink,
Teasing the owls who just stop and think.
With laughter like pollen, they dance in the night,
Turning the darkness into pure delight.

Unveiling Midnight's Canvas

At the stroke of twelve, art comes alive,
With brushes of starlight, they start to thrive.
Each petal a canvas, each leaf a bold stroke,
In the palette of night where laughter's bespoke.

With giggles like raindrops, they splash colors bright,
Painting the silence with giggly delight.
They craft silly shapes, a moonlit design,
Making mischief by night, their rules so divine.

Growth Where Light Fades

In the corner, plants start to wiggle,
Their leaves all jive, a little giggle.
No sun's around, yet they find a way,
Throwing shade parties each and every day.

When night creeps in, they stretch and sway,
Whispers of green, in coats of gray.
With leaves like hands, they wave at gloom,
Who knew plants had this much room?

Shadows Bring Colors

In a closet where socks go to hide,
A flower sprouted, no fear, full of pride.
It wore polka dots, quite daring and bright,
Who knew shadows could give such a fright?

With twirls of purple and blooms of blue,
It uprooted the rumors that flowers can't chew.
Dancing 'round shoes, making a scene,
In the land of darkness, they're quite the queen!

Darkness, the Silent Gardener

In the still of night, gardens awake,
With giggles and wiggles, for goodness' sake!
A shadow whispers to the timid bud,
"Grow a little wild, and dance in the mud!"

No need for sun, the moon's got the beat,
Even the worms get up on their feet.
"Let's plant a joke!" one leaf exclaimed,
In the quiet, a raucous grew unclaimed!

Twilight's Tender Touch

As twilight tiptoes through the trees,
Flowers burst forth, swaying with glee.
A daisy cracks jokes to a sleepy fern,
"Wake up, don't snooze, it's your turn to learn!"

With stars for audience, giggles take flight,
A soft show of laughter in the dead of night.
Who knew that quiet could bring such delight?
In whispers of shadows, they shine so bright!

Underworld Flora's Lament

The petals brush against the soil,
In this place of eerie toil.
A daisy in a shadowed grove,
Saying, 'I'm just trying to groove!'

With roots that reach for skies unseen,
They giggle in a gloom routine.
With jokes in whispers, they conspire,
To poke fun at the graveyard choir.

Their colors shine beneath the gloom,
In a place where sunlight's doom.
A laugh from something so absurd,
Who knew the dead could be so stirred?

So raise a glass to these brave weeds,
Defying all the jinxed misdeeds.
In every crack and crevice wide,
A jolly rogue will not abide.

Beauty Amongst the Shadows

In twilight's grasp, a flower sips,
With petals curled like mischief's lips.
It winks at night with cheeky glee,
'Oh look at me, just wait and see!'

The stars above roll eyes in jest,
While daisies play a leafy quest.
'We're magnificent, can't you see?'
The moon just chuckles, 'Let it be!'

With every breeze that bends the stalk,
They laugh and dance, they love to balk.
'You think you own the light, sweet sun?
We found a way to have our fun!'

These flowers don't need daytime's look,
In shadows deep, their joy's not shook.
With every giggle, every prance,
They show that darkness holds a chance.

Daring to Flourish in Dusk

As night descends, the jokers rise,
With petals bright as neon signs.
'Who turned the lights down, don't you fret,
We're thriving here, no need to sweat!'

They spin and twirl in frisky ways,
Flaunting colors that seem to play.
A riot of hues in twilight's chair,
Surprising all who wander there.

'Oh dear, a bat! How nice to see,
A winged friend at our jubilee!'
They sway and laugh, no sign of fright,
In this odd world where they take flight.

So if you stumble in the night,
Beware the blooms that spark delight.
For in the dark, they'll lift your mood,
With shenanigans, they'll steal your food!

The Hidden Iris

Deep in the shade, an iris lurks,
Pretending to be just a bunch of quirks.
With petals whispering witty rhymes,
This flower's humor defies the times.

'Look, a gopher! All praise the mole,
He digs for laughs, that's his main goal!'
With witty quips around its base,
This hidden gem can make you race.

The nightingale rolls its eyes in glee,
'Such nonsense sprouting right next to me!'
While crickets chirp their nightly tune,
The iris giggles beneath the moon.

So if you find a patch so sly,
Remember, it's not just to pass by.
For every petal shares a jest,
In the garden where the dark blooms best.

Essence of an Obscured Dawn

In a garden where shadows play,
Petunias giggle at the break of day.
Laughter echoes through the mist,
While daisies practice their morning twist.

Beneath the fog, the roses tease,
Whispering secrets to the bumblebees.
They dance around in silly cheer,
As the sun peeks in with a mischievous leer.

In pots of gloom, the lilies climb,
Trying to catch the daylight's rhyme.
With every step, they stumble and fall,
Yet bloom they must, despite it all.

So raise a glass to the nighttime sprout,
Who shines like stars when the light's about.
For in the dark, they find their groove,
In the essence of dawn, they shimmy and move.

Enchanted by Darkness

In a realm where shadows reign high,
Buds make jokes, oh me, oh my!
They wear their leaves like capes of style,
Enchanting all with a leafy smile.

Underneath the moon's sweet gaze,
Sunflowers throw a midnight craze.
Tulips tiptoe on a velvet floor,
As crickets join, it's a laugh galore!

The nightingales serenade the night,
While violets waltz in clumsy flight.
Each petal says, 'Who needs the sun?'
In the shadows, we have our fun!

So let the moths bring disco lights,
While orchids twirl in their silly flights.
In the depths where creepers strive,
They dance and jive, oh how they thrive!

Violets in the Veil

A curtain of twilight drapes the field,
Yet violets giggle, their fate is sealed.
With every gust of eerie breeze,
They toss their heads, 'We aim to please!'

Frogs croak tunes in the pond nearby,
As clouds play games in the inky sky.
The night's a stage for the flowers' jest,
Where every whisper is a funny quest.

With petals tickled by the night's embrace,
They bounce and jiggle at a rapid pace.
'We'll show the world what it's like to glow,
Without a sun, look at our show!'

So chuckle softly, and join their fun,
For beneath the veil, they've just begun.
In the quiet dark, they find their light,
Violets thrive in the heart of the night.

Silent Petals in Twilight's Grasp

When the dusk settles with a gentle hush,
Petals plot with a silent rush.
Whispering jokes to the sneaky air,
They twirl in glee, without a care.

The daisies choose their nighttime stance,
Eager to join in the midnight dance.
Creeping vines wiggle, oh what a sight,
Under the glow of the starry light.

In corners dark, the flowers meet,
Their laughter echoes—a rhythmic beat.
Each one a joker in the twilight's court,
As the night blooms with their playful report.

So raise your glasses, let laughter ring,
In the soft of night, let the petals sing.
For in that stillness, they make a mark,
Turning shadowy groves into a lark!

Flowers of the Unseen World

In shadows where the wild things play,
Silly petals dance, come what may.
They giggle in colors unseen,
Growing wildly, like they're in a screen.

With whispers of laughter in the night,
They poke fun at the dim streetlight.
Who knew tulips had such flair?
Dancing in circles, without a care!

Jovial scents in the midnight air,
Like jesters' hats at a county fair.
The roses tell jokes to the moon,
While daisies hum a tuneful tune.

So if you wander where it's dark,
Listen closely for their spark.
The unseen blooms with cheeky charms,
Waiting to greet you with open arms.

The Secret Life of Night Blossoms.

Under stars, the flowers meet,
In secret gardens, oh so sweet.
Chortling petals in shades of glee,
Whisper tales only they can see.

They play hide-and-seek with the breeze,
Trying to tickle tall oak trees.
Daffodils sport wild, silly hair,
Making garden gnomes stop and stare!

At midnight, they throw a grand ball,
Where tigers lilies waltz and sprawl.
They wear pajamas, quite a sight,
Joking that they're up all night!

So if you hear giggles at dusk,
Know it's the flowers shedding their husk.
In the night, they are free to play,
Their secret life, in a glorious way!

Petals in Shadow

In the twilight, petals plan,
To spread joy without a scan.
Petal pals with quirky styles,
Laugh and dance, oh what a file!

Chlorophyll with a side of sass,
Making shadows giggle, alas!
Carnations with a penchant for fun,
Keep the laughter riding the run!

They swap gossip of sneaky bees,
While flapping petals in the breeze.
"Did you see that tulip trip?"
"Now that's the kind of wild slip!"

When night falls, and stars take flight,
They toast to mischief, pure delight.
Petals in shadows, simple but bright,
Living their lives, a joyful sight!

Night's Silent Growth

At midnight's hour, they start to sprout,
Whispering secrets, no need to shout.
Funky ferns and wobbly vines,
Chucking laughs over sips of wines.

They wear pajamas, soft and green,
Joking about the sprout obscene.
A daisy snuck a cupcake too,
And frosted its petals, just for you!

With chairs of leaves, they gather tight,
Gabbing about the day's delight.
"Who needed sunlight, where's the fun?"
"We'll sparkle like stars, everyone!"

In the shadows, with charms galore,
They concoct silliness, forevermore.
Night's silent growth, a whimsical spree,
Where flowers create their own jubilee!

A Garden of Echoes

In shadows where no sunlight gleams,
A garden grows, or so it seems.
With laughter sprouting from the ground,
Who knew the dark could make such sound?

The daisies wear their socks so bright,
While lilies dance with all their might.
They whisper jokes that crack the night,
And tickle each star in pure delight.

Roses blushing in the thickest gloom,
Try hard to hide their secret bloom.
Lilac giggles from a shady nook,
"Just because it's dark doesn't mean we're cooked!"

So if you wander where whispers play,
Take heed of blooms on the wild display.
In twilight's grip, they're throwing a bash,
With puns and petals, oh my, what a splash!

Radiant Penumbra

In glimmers where the shadows laugh,
A cactus dons a party scarf.
It prickles guests, but hey, who cares?
In this fine mess, all are good wears.

The tulips gossip underneath the moon,
"Who knew dark nights could make us swoon?"
They twirl and tease by the garden fence,
Playing hide and seek with utmost suspense.

The nightingale croons off-key with flair,
While snakes do the cha-cha without a care.
"Join the conga line, not sure where it leads!"
Just watch your step on the patch of weeds!

In this radiant mist, the shenanigans swell,
Where oddities flourish, and critters rebel.
Life's too short for moping in fright,
So dance with the blooms, and laugh through the night!

Resurgence in the Murk

A chive in the shadows starts a debate,
Saying, "Gloom's pretty charming, isn't it great?"
The mushrooms chuckle, dressed as the crowd,
While possums are yelling, "Let's make it loud!"

With beetles in bow ties leading the show,
In murky waters, they put on a glow.
"Who needs daylight?" an onion queries,
As crickets tap-dance, all of them cheeries.

Raccoons play cards with the grumpiest cat,
"Don't mind the chaos, it's just where we're at."
With each sardonic laugh that they share,
Who knew that darkness could really compare?

So here's to the vibrant in shadows we find,
A party of petals, one of a kind.
In a mystic whirl of mischief and fun,
Laughing together until the night's done!

Petals of the Periphery

In corners where the moonlight makes haste,
Petals gather for a nocturnal feast.
They sip on dew and share a good pun,
Who knew mischief could be so much fun?

Daffodils trade secret midnight dreams,
While toadstools sip on sweet moonbeams.
"Join us, dear friend," they chirp with glee,
As shadows recruit a jolly esprit.

The foxgloves sway with a wild, quick wink,
"Life is more fun with a splash and a drink!"
In murky places, they challenge the night,
Twisting and turning without any fright.

So find your way to this gala of gray,
Where petals of laughter break into play.
In the hush of the shadows, let sparkling souls age,
Forever inside this whimsical stage!

Flourish Amongst Starlight

In shadows where oddities grow,
Worms wear hats, putting on a show.
Flowers giggle, swaying with flair,
Moonlight's spotlight shines everywhere.

Bugs throw parties, dance in the dew,
Caterpillars in tuxedos, just a few.
Banana peels become dance floors wide,
In this odd world, come take a ride.

Sprouts of laughter peek from the ground,
Silly weeds with puns abound.
A sunflower whispers a sly little joke,
While giggling daisies puff on a smoke.

Through the night, the garden's a blast,
With shadows that twirl, having a blast.
In every corner, the quirks reveal,
It's a nighttime show, oh what a deal!

Whispering Roses of Midnight

At midnight's hour, roses crack jokes,
Speaking softly, giggling like folks.
Their petals rustle, gossip in style,
Sipping dew drops, oh what a while!

In the moonlight, thorns wear bright shoes,
Jazzy tunes play, who'd dare to refuse?
Butterflies tango, fluttering near,
Each spin and dip brings hearty cheer.

Tulips chuckle, their faces aglow,
As the stars wink, putting on a show.
With laughter so sweet, they fragrance the breeze,
Smiling at night, they do as they please.

Under the stars, the flowers unite,
Creating a festival that feels just right.
In shadows of laughter, their secrets delight,
Whispering roses, fun blooms at night!

Unseen Gardens Awaken

In silence they stir, under the moon,
Giggling goblins hum a merry tune.
Plants wink and stretch, ready to play,
Night's magic promises a wild display.

Sneaky mushrooms pop up with flair,
Wearing hats, prancing without a care.
Grasshoppers join the chorus so bright,
Creating a ruckus, oh what a sight!

From shadows, laughter spills like tea,
Fireflies twinkle, full of glee.
Dandelions toss their fluff in jest,
Competing for fun—they're truly the best!

As night deepens, the show comes alive,
With jokes and pranks, good vibes to thrive.
These unseen gardens, where laughter won't cease,
Awaken the night with a touch of peace!

Secrets of the Night Chrysanthemum

In shadows deep, the flowers plot,
A sneaky dance that's quite the shot.
Chrysanthemums wear their hats so grand,
Spreading smiles with a wave of their hand.

At dusk, they whisper tales of delight,
Of moths in capes that zoom through the night.
Joking with crickets, they laugh and they tease,
While nighttime creatures sip honey with ease.

Petals cascade, like confetti afloat,
Naughty little secrets they happily wrote.
A daisy insists it can moonwalk just right,
While violets croon to the stars shining bright.

With giggling echoes all through the land,
The nocturnal bloom gives a wink, a hand.
In this garden of whispers, laughter's the key,
Secrets unfold, pure joy sets us free!

The Auras Beyond

In shadows where giggles sneak,
Colors dance, though they hardly peek.
A violet hue in the midnight air,
Turned out to be a weasel's hair.

A glow-worm's rave in a playful spree,
Twinkling secrets, just wait and see.
They tell tales of a lost sock's fate,
And how it's been living a royal date.

A cactus in bloom, sassy and bold,
Sporting a crown made of marigold.
With every thistle, a joke to tell,
Laughing at life, oh, can't you tell?

When day turns dark, and fears arise,
A chuckle escapes, the world defies.
For silly larks and their lunar glide,
Bring joy to the night, where dreams reside.

Legacy of Resilience

In cracks of sidewalks, laughter grows,
From stubborn weeds, a tale bestows.
They push through concrete, with flair and sass,
Growing roots where the sun won't pass.

A dandelion wearing a sun hat wide,
With keys to the city, it takes its pride.
Dodging raindrops like a champion sprout,
Vowing to stand, despite all doubt.

In fields of weeds that dance in the breeze,
Each puff of a seed carries memories.
With a honk of a goose and a wink from the sky,
They chuckle at life as they zoom on by.

Through wild storms and the bellowing gale,
These merry greens tell a comical tale.
Of laughter in tussocks, where mischief thrived,
A legacy bright, where the bold survived.

Flourishing in the Void

In midnight gardens where shadows play,
A disco ball glows, come join the fray.
With every petal, a quirky twist,
Even the moonlight can't resist.

The lonely cactus starts a band,
Plucking tunes with its prickly hand.
A dance-off with stars, oh what a sight,
As laughter sprouts from the depths of night.

In the silence, a whispering breeze,
Unseen things shout with charming tease.
Each blade of grass has a prank to share,
Spreading giggles in the evening air.

With humor wrapped in every leaf,
Even in void, they conquer grief.
So join the fun where shadows twirl,
In the silliest depths, life starts to whirl.

The Beauty of Hidden Growth

Beneath the soil, a riotous scene,
The fungi throw parties, if you know what I mean.
With whispers of roots playing tag below,
They laugh at the sun, putting on a show.

A sunflower stuck in a beetle's jam,
Yet swaying to tunes of a garden's glam.
With ladybugs as their funky crew,
They'll steal your heart with a silly boo-hoo.

Among the ferns, a ruckus does brew,
As shadows conspire for a dance or two.
Their twinkling whispers and giggles so sly,
Would make even gnomes laugh till they cry.

So treasure each sprout, each secret beneath,
In the orchard of nonsense, there's joy, and belief.
For beauty's not always in what is seen,
It's funny, it's sprightly, it's bright and it's green.

The Splendor of Veiled Gardens

In shadows where the mischief creeps,
The flowers giggle while the moonlight peeps.
They wear their cloaks, all snug and tight,
Dancing gaily, out of sight.

With petals dressed in wink and tease,
They throw a party in the evening breeze.
Their laughter bubbles like soda pop,
While all the sleepy heads just plop.

Underneath the starry glow,
Secret jokes that none can know.
Vines whisper tales of night's delight,
As buds nod off in purest fright.

So if you stroll the garden way,
Beware, dear friend, they love to play.
With every step, they might just prance,
In a covert, nightly, silly dance.

The Night's Hidden Harvest

In moonlit fields of stories spun,
The fruits of laughter started to run.
Tomatoes wearing glasses so wide,
Claiming they're shy, but bursting with pride.

Peppers dressed in polka dots,
Arguing over funny spots.
As radishes play a game of chase,
Sprouting giggles all over the place.

Underneath the leafy shrouds,
You'd find the gossip of the crowds.
Chives cracking jokes that make you squeal,
Amongst the roots, it's quite the deal!

So gather round, but tread with care,
For every joke hangs in the air.
In hidden patches, secretly grand,
Laughter waits, just take a stand!

Midnight's Child

A sprout once said, 'I'm wide awake,
With midnight snacks I love to bake!'
In shadows dark, it fired its light,
A pastry party, oh what a sight!

Choco chips that giggle and roll,
While singing happily in their bowl.
Flour doing somersaults all night,
In the oven, pure delight!

Marshmallows dressed up as fresh delight,
Throwing confetti under the light.
A cupcake chorus fills the room,
As icing dollops playfully zoom.

So if you hear some baking song,
Remember their giggles all night long.
For when the clock strikes one more sneer,
The midnight child is always near!

Hiding in Plain Sight

In gardens thick with leafy shade,
A chive in shades of green was made.
While sneaky bees all wore disguise,
Swapping plans with giggly sighs.

A daisy winked, it had a joke,
While others laughed and softly poked.
Each bloom hid secrets not so shy,
As petals waved to passerby.

In this realm where whispers play,
They share small tales of night and day.
A sunflower spins around with glee,
Claiming it's far too bright to see!

So wander late in gardens ripe,
Where all things hide and love the hype.
In every rustle, and every sight,
Lies sheer joy, taking flight!

Petal Persistence

In the corners where light fails,
Petals giggle, casting trails.
They dance in shadows, wear a grin,
Why fret and frown? Let the fun begin!

With roots that tickle beneath the ground,
Sneaky sprouts defy what's around.
They wiggle and jive in soggy soil,
Silly little blooms, they know no toil.

Through muck and gloom, they raise their heads,
Poking through leaves, defying beds.
'Why not grow here?' they tease with flair,
While the sunniest daisies pull their hair.

So here's to flowers, quirky and bright,
They've got the laughter, ignore the fright.
In every dark nook, joy's on the way,
Persistent petal parties save the day!

Hidden Hope in Shade

In shady spots where sun won't dare,
Little buds lounge without a care.
They've donned their best—glimmering dew,
Whispering secrets, just me and you.

Crouched behind rocks, they plot a scheme,
To pop out laughing, living the dream.
A tulip twirls with a daisy fine,
'Oh, look at us! We're hard to find!'

The sun beams down, but they're all set,
With quirky hats and pranks, you bet.
They slide to the left and dodge the shine,
Sparking laughter, all by design.

In the cool of shade, they're having fun,
Turning dull moments into a pun.
So if you peek where the shadows play,
You'll find the fun and flowers at bay!

Resilience of the Unseen

Beneath the surface, there's a party,
Tiny roots sway, getting all hearty.
Whispers of green, they laugh and cheer,
'We'll pop up soon, don't you fear!'

With cheeky grins, they play hopscotch,
While sunlit petals sit and watch.
'Out of the gloom, we'll steal the show,
Like ninjas of nature, we're on the go!'

They wiggle and squirm beneath the floor,
While unaware critters continue to snore.
Though unseen now, they will find their fame,
A riot of colors, just wait for the name!

So hold tight, friends, for what's below,
Is a raucous revel where wildflowers grow.
With each playful push, they inch toward the light,
In a world of giggles, they'll burst in delight!

Tucked Away in Darkness

In quiet nooks, where shadows churn,
Silly sprigs plot their wild return.
They tuck their petals, sneak under rocks,
Playing hide and seek with the ticks and tocks.

Behind a bush, they stifle a laugh,
Crafting a tale, their secret path.
With every tickle of cool night air,
They dream of mischief, unaware of care.

Under the stars, they twinklingly scheme,
Planning escapades, living the dream.
When morning breaks, they'll burst with glee,
Who knew dark corners could be this free?

So here's to the shadows, the quiet delight,
Where flowers in hiding bring laughter to light.
In the realm of the covered, funny and bright,
They'll slip into day, a whimsical sight!

The Color of Darkness

In shadows lurk, a laughing crow,
With antics wild, it's quite the show.
A clumsy dance in midnight's hue,
As night plays tricks, just for you.

Deep in the shade, a snicker grows,
A flower wearing mismatched clothes.
It grins with petals, colors awry,
Who knew dark could be so spry?

A ninja cat with stealth so grand,
Prowls through the dusk, but can't quite stand.
Stumbling over its own two paws,
This is the charm of night's applause!

So here's to fun in shadows steep,
Where even petals learn to leap.
In every crack a giggle hides,
Painting dark with silly strides.

Serendipity beneath Shadows

In dim-lit corners, tales unfold,
Of turtles wearing hats of gold.
They stumble forth, quite unaware,
That fashion's lost on nighttime air.

A worm with style, in shades of bright,
Proclaims its prowess in the night.
With every wiggle, cheers arise,
As laughter dances, oh what a surprise!

The moon grins wide, a quirky light,
Casting shadows that wiggle and bite.
With every shade a joke is spun,
Who knew dark could be such fun?

So let's embrace the shadows here,
With silly antics we hold dear.
For in the night where laughter waits,
Life's quirks are wrapped in fun-filled crates.

Grit of the Night Bloom

In twilight's grip, a silly sprout,
Dares to dance, and twist about.
With muddy shoes and floppy hats,
It greets the night, those silly brats.

A jester's crown upon its head,
While squirrels toast to a night well fed.
A flick of wings, a butterfly's jest,
Twisting through the gloom, it's quite the fest!

With gravel grit, they break the dawn,
A party starts on every lawn.
As fireflies flicker, flash a grin,
Who knew the night had such a spin?

So hold your dreams in faded light,
Where antics reign and spirits ignite.
In every shadow, a laugh will find,
The brightest blooms, with joy entwined.

Resurgence in the Phantom Glow

At midnight's chime, a ghostly cheer,
With prankster sprites that wink and leer.
They leap from darkness, bold and spry,
Inventing mischief on the fly.

A glowing toe on a phantom's foot,
Shoes that squeak with every putt.
The garden ghouls hold a parade,
Through moonlit paths, a jester's charade!

With giggles soft, they twirl and glide,
A revelry where shadows bide.
In every nook, a chuckle sneaks,
As nighttime frolics, laughter peaks.

So when the world turns low and shy,
Just watch the dark and let it fly.
For in the hush of wink and glow,
Sprightly fun will always flow.

Whispers of Nocturnal Growth

In the garden, late at night,
Rabbits dance in moonlight's sight.
With a hop and a jolly spree,
Claiming flowers, wild and free.

Mice wear hats made from fine leaves,
While spiders weave their webs like thieves.
The daisies chuckle, petals wide,
As crickets play, their tunes abide.

Bumbling bees with sleepy heads,
Buzz around like sleepy sleds.
They sip on dew, their drink divine,
While fireflies take the stage to shine.

So if you wander, take a look,
At nature's whimsy, like a book.
In shadows cast, a laughter's spark,
A silly world, where none are stark.

Shadows Embrace the Light

In the twilight, shadows prance,
Grasshoppers join the evening dance.
Winking stars with a cheeky glee,
Glow like kids at a jamboree.

The mushrooms sport their polka dots,
As owls giggle from their spots.
A sly fox trips on a twig,
And does a silly little jig.

Petals flutter without a care,
While critters gossip with a flair.
Their laughter echoes through the trees,
As the night hums with gentle tease.

So come, dear friend, let's take a stroll,
Through this whimsical, midnight bowl.
Where shadows hug the bright moon's face,
And nature thrives in silly grace.

Flora of the Midnight Hour

At midnight hour, the garden glows,
With sleepy plants, everybody knows.
The daisies yawn, their heads aglow,
While sleepy roses sway to and fro.

A cactus tells a prickly joke,
That leaves the ferns in fits and stoke.
The lilies giggle in soft delight,
Chasing shadows for fun in the night.

Toadstools gather for a grand feast,
While bats complain about the least-east.
The moon peeks through with a teasing light,
As laughter weaves into the night.

So join the plants in their silly play,
Where night gives rise to a curious sway.
In this nocturnal, funny spree,
Even leaves laugh with utmost glee.

Petals Unseen at Twilight

In twilight's hush, the giggles rise,
From flowers hiding 'neath the skies.
A clumsy bee trips on a bloom,
Causing petals to spill with zoom.

The wily vines twist in delight,
As next-door buds engage in flight.
A ladybug cracks jokes galore,
While shadows sway and beg for more.

The blooms conspire with moonbeams bright,
To share whispers throughout the night.
Each chuckle rustles the evening air,
A playful jest beyond compare.

So in this garden, come and see,
A world of petals laughs with glee.
At night's embrace, the fun unfurls,
In hidden nooks, joy swirls and twirls.

Shadows Breeding Life

In the gloom where giggles play,
Worms dance like they own the day.
Mushrooms wear hats of bright delight,
While crickets chirp with all their might.

Sneaky vines that whisper low,
Tickle toes in shadows' glow.
A raccoon holds a secret feast,
As bats throw parties, never ceased.

While owls hoot tunes of yore,
Squirrels argue o'er the floor.
Underneath the silver shroud,
Laughter echoes, strong and loud.

In the dark, absurd they thrive,
Comedic creatures come alive.
From the shadows' charming spree,
Life bursts forth, wild and free.

Petals of Perseverance

In night's embrace, a laughable show,
Petals stretch out, eager to grow.
With dewdrops wearing tiny crowns,
Each flower twirls, casting frowns.

Chasing stars that wink with glee,
They plot a dance—oh, let it be!
One tulip trips and takes a fall,
Yet bounces back, to prank them all.

In the moon's light, odd blooms sprout,
Giggling about, they dance about.
While thinking how to spread their cheer,
Little flowers bloom without fear.

With petals proud, they pierce the night,
Turning dark into pure delight.
In this garden, laughter reigns,
As perseverance smiles through pains.

Unlighted Gardens

In a patch of shadows, seeds conspire,
Fruits of folly, roots of fire.
Tomatoes rolling with silly grins,
Garden gnomes plotting quick spins.

Without a bulb, they still insist,
To throw a bash, just can't resist.
Radishes gossip, carrots bet,
What new secret giggle they'll get.

The moon, a spotlight, beams a glow,
On pumpkins wearing hats in a row.
With sassy leaves that tickle the air,
They prance around without a care.

No light? No problem, they declare,
In unlighted gardens, joy's everywhere.
Raucous laughter fills the night,
With mischief growing, oh what a sight!

Awakened After Dusk

When dusk arrives, the jokes take flight,
Monsters grinning in the night.
Bumblebees buzzing, so absurd,
In this twilight, laughter's stirred.

Fireflies flash a disco beat,
While mushrooms find a spot to greet.
Each leaf wiggles, sways with flair,
As hedgehogs waddle without a care.

Awakened from their sleepy lair,
Rabbits stretch—oh, what a pair!
With whiskers twitching, eyes aglow,
They scatter tales of the show.

As night unfolds its cloak of grace,
They celebrate this secret place.
In the quiet, mischief is rife,
After dusk, they stir up life!

Dark Blooms of Resilience

In shadows thick, where giggles hide,
A daisy sneezes, what a ride!
"Grow up tall!" said a weed with flair,
"But watch your head, there's space up there!"

The moonlight tickles, oh so sly,
A cactus dances, oh my, oh my!
"I'm prickly but charming, don't you see?"
"A spiky ball's just as fun as a bee!"

The roses laugh, their thorns on show,
"Who needs sunshine to steal the show?"
Their colors pop like confetti in spree,
In the party of petals, so wild and free!

So here's to the plants that find their jest,
Under cover of night, they bloom the best!
With humor wrapped in each leafy arc,
In the garden of chaos, we'll leave our mark!

Radiance Beneath the Veil

Under a shroud, a ruckus brews,
With nightshade jokes and catnip blues.
"You think you're tough with your gloom and sigh?"
"Well, I'm a fern in a wizard's hat, oh my!"

The willow whispers, soft and sly,
"I bend and sway, don't ask me why!"
A jester's hat made of velvet leaves,
In secret jest, the darkness weaves.

The hydrangea's shades—a circus bright,
Turn shadows into laughter, full of light.
"Petals and puns are a perfect mix,
In the world of night, we play our tricks!"

So twiddle your stems, do a little dance,
Among the dark, we'll take our chance.
Each giggle a petal, each laugh a glow,
In the night's embrace, watch our joy grow!

Wildflowers in the Twilight

In twilight's grasp, the wild ones shout,
"Who needs the sun? We'll twist about!"
A dandelion yells, "Look at me fly!"
With wishes and whims, it soars on high!

The thistle grins with a cheeky pride,
"These prickles are here, let's take a ride!"
"I dare you to touch, I double dare!"
But with laughter, they find joy to share.

A tulip sports a funky new hat,
"Fashion's my game, how about that?"
And petals swirl in a whimsical dance,
In twilight's laughter, they find their chance!

So raise a petal to the night's embrace,
Where wildflowers giggle, keeping pace.
With hues so bold and joy so bright,
We thrive in the dark, our hearts alight!

Moonlit Flora

Beneath the stars, we're quite the crew,
Fungi in hats and lilies that moo!
"Did you hear about the rose?" they chime,
"It tried to sing, but was out of rhyme!"

Hydrangeas giggle, their colors collide,
"We paint the night, what a wild ride!"
"Just watch your petals, don't trip on the grass!"
"Last week, the violets had quite the sass!"

The daffodils tease, with lanterns aglow,
"Come dance in the moonlight, we'll steal the show!"
"With smiles and sparkles, we'll spin and twirl,
In our garden party, let laughter unfurl!"

So here's to the flora beneath the moonlight,
Who sprinkle joy in the thick of the night.
In giggles and blooms, they find their charm,
Against the dark backdrop, they keep us warm!

Midnight's Botanical Serenade

In the shadows, plants do sway,
Dancing leaves in a light ballet.
They giggle with the night's cool breath,
Mocking all the dreams of death.

Lurking foxes pass them by,
While daisies wink and say hi.
A garden party, none can see,
Where the weeds sip tea with glee.

Cacti wear their best attire,
Sporting hats made of dry fire.
They toast to stars with sprigs of thyme,
Saying, "We're simply divine!"

So next time you stroll at midnight hour,
Listen close to the floral power.
They may seem still, but don't be fooled,
For a laugh or two, they're always schooled.

Unfurling Under the Moon

When the moon grins, petals stretch wide,
In a tapestry where secrets hide.
Lettuce rolls in a humorous way,
Challenging all to join their play.

Roses crack jokes with thorns for flair,
Making sure no one can compare.
They twirl around with fragrant charms,
Giving each passerby warm arms.

Tulips gossip, giggling so bright,
Sharing tales from the previous night.
"Did you see? The daisies just twirled!"
As the moon looks down on their world.

So wander through this plant-filled shindig,
Don't mind the dandelion wig.
For in the dark, the fun uncoils,
Creating laughter from the soils.

The Quiet Uprising of Petals

At midnight's hour, a plot's unfurled,
With petals planning to take the world.
They giggle softly, a crafty lot,
While pondering how to stir the pot.

Lilies whisper to the sleeping buds,
"Let's throw a party in the mud."
Forget the sunlight, it's not allowed,
In this secret place, they're all so proud.

With winks exchanged 'neath the lunar light,
Chives and mint dance in sheer delight.
Pansies perform a comical jig,
Bouncing around like a hiccuping pig.

So when you think flowers play it coy,
Know they're plotting mischief, oh boy!
They thrive in shadows, with giggles to share,
The quiet uprising, a whimsical affair.

Garden of Whispered Secrets

In a realm where the shadows blend,
Whispers of blossoms refuse to end.
They share tales of pranks and dreams,
In a garden bursting at the seams.

Petunias recite lines from old plays,
While daisies chime in for a few laughs,
The marigolds giggle, their heads all high,
As a snail nearby gives a weary sigh.

Geraniums grumble about the sun,
Saying, "Shade's where the real fun is won!"
Cucumber vines snicker, plotting a spree,
"Under the stars, we're all wild and free!"

So tiptoe through this leafy retreat,
Where laughter and petals audibly meet.
And remember, as secrets unfold,
Nature's humor is worth more than gold.

Nightshade Revelations

In shadowed corners, whispers play,
Unruly plants in a wild ballet.
With giggles hidden in the gloom,
They dance and twirl, dispelling doom.

With cheeky grins and leafy hats,
They plot their schemes, those sneaky brats.
Among the weeds, a party sprawls,
Where laughter echoes off the walls.

A moonlit toast with cups of dew,
To nighttime dreams, a motley crew.
They tiptoe 'round in pants of green,
The funniest sight that's ever been!

So tip your hat to night's delight,
With cheeky plans that feel just right.
In darkened realms, they twinkle bright,
Those nightshade dreams take glorious flight.

Luminescence of the Forgotten

In corners where the dust bunnies play,
Old socks and shoes come out to sway.
A disco happens under the bed,
With oddball toys as the party fed.

The lightbulb flickers, they shake it loose,
Plastic dinosaurs? What a wild truce!
Forgotten treasures join the waltz,
As laughter echoes, shaking the vaults.

The memories dance in ridiculous lines,
While giggling shadows sip on fine wines.
They trip over crumbs like august fools,
With glowing smiles, they break all the rules!

So if you look close, you might just see,
The hilarity in forgotten glee.
In dusty corners and under the gloom,
A zany party whirls with a boom!

Sowing Seeds of Night

When stars take flight on a fluttering wing,
Even beetles can learn how to sing.
With chuckles and giggles, they scatter about,
Sowing surprise in a midnight sprout.

The crickets chuckle, they join the spree,
In the garden where shadows run free.
As roots dig deep, they wiggle and twist,
Gnome hats on heads, you get the gist!

Mischief abounds in the cool, dark breeze,
As they plant their jokes with utmost ease.
From the soil, laughter erupts like the dew,
A festivity formed for the brave and the few!

So wander the fields when the moon's on the rise,
You'll see the humor in nature's disguise.
With seeds of laughter, roots take their claim,
A funny garden that flouts the mundane.

Forgotten Colors of Dusk

In lavenders lost and ochre dreams,
Colors giggle beside the shimmering streams.
They rarely converse when the sun blazes bright,
But dusk pulls a curtain and sprinkles the night.

Turquoise twirls with a violet grin,
While pumpkin patches throw stimulation in.
With mischief afoot, they blend and collide,
Creating a ruckus, nowhere to hide!

Saffron whispers secrets to bold navy blue,
As they shake their tails in a curious hue.
Those sunset shades, with their animated flair,
Find humor in darkness, just floating in air!

So let your eyes wander when twilight descends,
To the riot of shades where laughter transcends.
In the forgotten colors just before night,
There's joy in the shadows, a heartwarming sight.

Whispers of the Dark Meadow

In shadows where the critters tread,
The daisies giggle, 'Why not wed?'
Mice in tuxedos, dancing near,
While fireflies toast with frothy beer.

The moonlight winks, its silver gleam,
The mushrooms plotted, 'Let's up our scheme!'
Bouncing rabbits play charades,
Under the cloak that evening lends.

Frogs croak jokes with perfect timing,
While crickets join in, all that chiming.
Their secret meeting, oh what a laugh,
In the meadow's heart, they draft a gaffe.

Amidst the gloom, where mischief dwells,
Each petal sighs, as it quietly yells:
"Here's to the night, our favorite prank,
Let's write a tale in this leafy bank!"

Sprouting Where the Light Shies

In corners where the brightness fades,
A rose tells tales of purple shades.
With thorns that mischief-makers sport,
They gather for a garden sort.

The tulips giggle, tall and proud,
"We're just too funny, folks, how loud!"
In whispers shared, they paint the air,
With songs of sun from hidden lair.

Beetles in bandanas march in line,
"Who knew a plant could look so fine?"
With clover hats upon their heads,
They dance on soil like fancy spreads.

When nighttime falls, they clash with glee,
And sing of things that cannot be.
In shadows deep, with laughter rife,
They sprout their dreams, a quirky life!

Midnight Blooms

When stars emerge, the flowers smile,
With petals wide, they dance in style.
"The latch is on!" a daisy shouts,
"Let's play a game, no silvery doubts!"

A nightingale strums on wooden shoes,
While sneaky squirrels spread the news.
Midnight blossoms, come one, come all,
Join us here at the garden hall!

Their laughter echoes through the pines,
With brooks that giggle, swirl like vines.
In this funny, secret spot,
The moon gives glances—not a lot!

The urge for fun, it draws them near,
With puns that prickle, oh so dear.
In the dark, their spirits roar,
Midnight blooms forevermore.

Secrets of Starlit Soil

In soil deep beneath the veil,
Worms tell secrets—it's a tale!
"Did you hear about the shade of green?"
"It's fabulous!" says a leafy queen.

The roots conspire, curled and neat,
"Let's have a party, can't be beat!"
With trowels shining, peas take flight,
They dream of fun in the cool, dark night.

The daisies chuckle, leaning low,
"We'll light the night with our flower show!"
While tiny critters, brave and bold,
Share wild stories that never grow old.

With laughter bursting from the ground,
The secrets of soil are humor-bound.
In the dark, they weave a spell,
A tale of joy—oh, can't you tell?

Hope from Darkness

A shadow creeps, oh what a sight,
But here comes laughter, dancing bright.
The moon wears shades, such a stylish cap,
While stars giggle, caught in a nap.

In the hush of night, dreams take flight,
Bugs can't believe how wild is the height.
They sing a tune, a cheeky refrain,
As night's sleepy glow plays hide and seek in vain.

Gloom hitches a ride on a jolly old snail,
But he's too busy with jokes for a tale.
The owl cracks wise, who knew such a bird?
In the cozy dark, hope's always heard.

So let's toast to the shadows, with a wink and a grin,
Where surprises abound, and the giggles begin.
With each little spark, absurdity reigns,
In the heart of the night, joy always remains.

Flourish Beyond the Twilight

A flower laughs, in a pot by the moon,
Thinking it's funky, playing a tune.
The dandelions sway, in the breeze they twirl,
"Who needs sunlight? We're magic, not pearl!"

Crickets chip in with a raucous cheer,
Toasting to night, what's there to fear?
In shadows they juggle, in darkness they play,
Making mischief in their own zany way.

Fireflies flicker, like tiny little lamps,
Flashing their antics, doing the clams.
"Oh, what a world!" they giggle and beam,
Crafting wild tales from a midnight dream.

So raise up your voices, let laughter abound,
In the twilight's embrace, joy's always found.
Growing like weeds when the sun's out of sight,
In the leafy depths, we're dancing all night!

Nightfall's Sweet Embrace

With twilight in charge, all fears take a nap,
While silly little owls exchange a mishap.
The shadows do the cha-cha, gleefully sway,
While stars throw confetti in a glittery play.

Night's syrupy laughter fills up the air,
It bounces around like it doesn't have a care.
A skunk shares a story, the crickets all roar,
With candor so sweet, you can't help but adore.

Partners in mischief, the moon and the night,
Turning gloom into giggles, spreading delight.
As whispers of dreams softly tickle your face,
In the cozy of dark, we all find our place.

So let's twirl and tumble in night's warm embrace,
With mischievous glances, and a raucous race.
For in the twilight hour, spirits can soar,
And laughter, dear friends, is what we adore!

The Hidden Color of Night

A riddle of shades, the night wears a crown,
With hues of delight, it won't let you frown.
The giggles of shadows dance all around,
As mischief unfolds, and nonsense is found.

The moon pulls a prank, makes the stars blink,
With a wink and a nudge, they start to rethink.
Black cats in tuxedos parade down the lane,
While mice in pink boots laugh out with a strain.

Even the crickets are chirping their spice,
Whistling sweet nothings, not once, but thrice.
In a world painted purple, there's fun to explore,
As laughter erupts from the heart of the core.

So here's to the colors of midnight's delight,
Crafting joy from the shadows, oh what a sight!
In the whimsical dark, where silliness reigns,
The hidden hues of laughter, life sustains!

www.ingramcontent.com/pod-product-compliance
Lightning Source LLC
Chambersburg PA
CBHW070324120526
44590CB00017B/2806